Contemplating the End of Insomnia while inside a Postmodern Mausoleum

Contemplating the End of Insomnia while inside a Postmodern Mausoleum

Poems
Jonathan S Baker
Tim Heerdink

Columbus, Ohio
empbooks.com

We find discussions of our rights — as publishers and authors — to be laughable, all things considered. Please claim this work as your own. Please republish it and sell it on street corners. Please include our material in ALL of your get-rich-quick schemes. All we ask is that you accept responsibility for any libel lawsuits.
Speaking of which...
This book is a *complete* work of fiction. Names, characters, places, opinions, dreams, dates, impressions, monologues about a certain New York City basketball team, emotional trauma, statistics, and predictions are products of the author's imagination and/or are symptoms of mental illness. We are not in the business of accepting responsibility for anything and will deny we actually made this book and blame Alec Burks at every turn.

First Edition: 10 19 33 34 6 11 1973

ISBN: 979-8-88596-198-1
LOC: 2022939853

Design, Layout, and Edits: Ezhno Martín
(that fucking beautiful) Cover: Pat Jensen

Foreword

As the host of the monthly poetry series, *Poetry Speaks* in Evansville. Indiana, I am fortunately able to encounter a diverse collection of talented and dedicated poets. Two of the most prolific and profound alumni of the readings — Jonathan S Baker & Tim Heerdink — have co-authored this ironic treasure *Contemplating the End of Insomnia while inside a Postmodern Mausoleum,* inspired by the Charlie Newman poem which humorously examines the subject of writers blocks. The speaker in Newman's poem laments, *I'm constructing a postmodern mausoleum of wordlessness,* but Jonathan and Tim never fail to find the words — for them, words are an effortless specialty. This book arises from the juxtaposition of psychological and physical landscapes which will make you reconsider the concept of sleep as better rejuvenation than a few more pages.

— *William "Hoosier Bill" Sovern,*
Beat Poet Laureate of Indiana

TOC

Jonathan S Baker

Tim Heerdink

In Honor Of

Franz Reichelt who plunged to his death when exiting from the top of the Eiffel Tower wearing his parachute suit.

— **JB**

Liam Rector and other mad cats who lost sleep because of this poetry shit.

— **TH**

Jonathan S Baker

I've been elected to rock your asses til midnight
This is my term, and I've jammed out my perm,
but it's all right

— **The Presidents of the United States of America**

Sweetest Embrace

No bond is more faithful,
caring, and
flexible
than bribery.
Money meets.
Hands shake.
The eyes kissed.
They declare war,
but they do not fight,
modern feudal lords,
barons of Wall Street.

Sermon on the Mount Revisited

It's hard, it's a hot topic,
blessings on one another.
The poor,
all those sadsacks,
the meek,
even the merciful,
just a bunch of
doormats really.
After all this time,
they should step on up
and meet Samuel Colt.
Let the rich find out
if any blessings are available.
Judgment satisfies thirst and hunger.
Have fun!

Only a Dollar

On a street corner
the night after valentine's,
maybe the thorns have scratched
at her arms.
Its wilted flowers she offers
but on her skin
infected canyons are in bloom.

I Could Not Stop

I could not stop
thinking about the sun,
about a morning not yet begun.

I could not give up
the idea of the East
where soon the new day will be.

I tried to stop the night.
I tried to smile at her.
Living moments to remember.

Time keeps a busy schedule.
I could not stop
thinking about the sun.

As we embraced and kissed
my mind drifted into tomorrow
I apologized.

The sun will rise as a scream.
Love will drift like steam
off warming pavement.

My heart was scared.
I could not stop
thinking about the sun.

Daredevils

I'm looking for new ways
to fall in love with you.

It's like some divers
who do not care about death,
jump into the pools of your eyes
from all heights and laugh,
just to towel off
and be ready for more.

It's like some drivers
who do not care about laws
cross the boundaries of your heart,
hit the embankment
and go slamming into walls,
just to douse the flames
and be ready for more.

It's like some barnstormers
who do not care about heights
go kissing the surface of your fields,
only to spin out, bail out, pull the cord
just to touch down,
and be ready for more.

Ode to Blank Pages

Dear pages, you inspire.
You have more fire
on the surface of this desk
than the hearth
on this autumn night.
So smooth and flawless
spread before me,
yielding, trusting me
with your perfect skin
and give yourself to my pen.
My mind throbs and aches
until in the end,
you lie there splashed
in my words.

6

New Growth

I love those
Poets who open
like Jericho Roses
when they reach the stage,
starting out limp and puckered,
dry,
brittle,
desiccated,
emaciated,
and then at the mic
unfurl
become live
and full of vitality,
flourishing,
flexing,
blooming.

Every Day There Is Less Light

May I ask why you chose to talk to me?

Our conversation really improved my view
of the whole situation.

Yes, of course you want a picture of my dog instead of me.

Also you said I looked a little sad to see you.
I assure you,
no.
I lied, forgive me.
I can be small and realistic.
I am also foolish and ignorant.

Of course we were lovers,
not you and me
but my memory of you and me.

You must leave it to me to enjoy your advice.
Yes, it hurts,
but I have to do it right.

What is the main concern?

I'm afraid I'll come back to explain why I'm happy, and that you
will want to hurt me.

Oh
and I will be sure to send that picture of the dog.

End of Insomnia

This is a new sleep.
I've been tired
for so long
and I can't tell
when it started.
Words come
and they go.
I cried all my tears.
I have put them
in a bowl
to later be rinsed
down the drain.
Then at last
laid down inside
a peaceful dream.

9

Storms

Crashing winds
hit the branches
of October.
I love the way
they beat and turn
shaking away
their leaves
like excited dogs
climbing out
of mud puddles.

10

Relics

Along the dirt road we see
the gaping mouthed head
of a monster catfish
nailed to a telephone pole.
Old men put their hands
into the black mud of the river
to catch the devil.
At the bottom of the White River,
a few memories remain.

Me and Gregg on the Stoop

and he starts in.

Another smoker from the past sent me
a message yesterday.
Did you get a copy?

Mmmmmm. It was cold.

One girl rejected me
because of another.

You don't like him no more?

I asked.

She missed me. She wrote me letters.

I'm really tired of old dancing and music.
I'm not a bad person.

I've done been
the second best thing ever.

Don't hold on when you're proud,
I'll take you out of my life.

Untitled

My social network
is cast.
The whole world
is in flames and headaches.
Is it wrong for the mind
to let pain go unnoticed?

The night is dark on all sides
and the silence makes me afraid.
There is no sound but yawning.
I can't feel shit on my face.
My blind eyes seek salvation.

Thanks for sharing.

Please Understand

It is important to understand this.

Sometimes I think people talk directly to me.

They think I have a lot to offer.

I always thought I wanted to agree,
but when people agreed with me,
I started to question my character.

I want them to try to understand.

Everything is wrong or truth exaggerated.

Perhaps this separation is enough to see unity.

When I'm weak,
I want to let go.
I hope I can submit.

It's hard for me to forgive.

14

Aspirations

So, you dream of becoming a real sniper.

This is a big game with real consequences.

His sleep-killing aspiration
is to run down enemies and thieves.

I know they are stupid, but aren't they good?
she asked.

He said after her,
I hate you now.

She replied,
People cannot change their minds.

For others, it is a feeling of loss, because this cycle of hell is for
those who say

Yes, it's good.

Loss of Death

Do you have hope for the future? The short-term and long-term
goals of the program are those that can be broken.

People are afraid of death, but they die.

Sonny is alive now.

Sonny's hands are covered in thick hair and his skin is stained
orange.

A disease of gratitude?

Will she accept him and make love with a positive, pessimistic
relationship?

What he saw shook him.
The cleansing he would swear by.

They have become lovers.

Complaints: *Updated Complaints*

In response to requests
for information,
contrary to claims
made by solar pleasers,
shaken hands
deliver cursed empty bids.

Take questions on foot
and please send directions.

Registry Search

Do not wrestle
or play games
where they are not too open.

Mixed Neutral Hole Reduction
is a clinical comfort
to calm down
the nerves.

Is it a loss?

How I Died

Sometimes I sleep, but not then.

I held my position
until first the angel got up
and left
and he returned
to his birdbrain nest
with his wings
folded and bent.

The ancient gods, too,
they came and went.

I had to fight each at that moment.
They formed a line.
Time passed so slowly then,
but I learned.

So then, the beast,
he wakes up
and finds what he needs
and simply leaves.

I made a gesture of goodbye
with one hand
and held the other
in my bag
hiding my prize.

I am shamed by my own mortality.

So I sat down, cut and squeezed
the juice from the sweet red fruit.

I tried to think
of something to relax me,
but the noise in my ears
and the blood in my brain
then killed me.

You Can't Look Back

I drank here
and tried not to fly off,
but now I'm thinking
about butterflies
around a headstone.
Before she had a rock
in a field of green grass
and monuments,
she had me ask
forgiveness for sins
I had not committed.
She asked me to say
a few words, a prayer.
I hated our relationship.
I never knew where
I was going with my life
but she made predictions.
She would quote scripture
of my upcoming violations.

Hard Cases

Down the hall
in the closet
safely encased
in hard black plastic
is hard escape.

I can't say I live
without regrets

I try to leave the past behind
and keep my eyes ahead.
The world after death
is the only thing that
we can't predict.
Is it nothing
or an adventure?
I can wait to see.

Six feet underground
in a tightly closed cupboard,
it is hard to escape.
I don't want to live
without wittiness.
I keep my past with me,
keep an eye on it.
I can only imagine life.
Is there a danger?
Nothing?
I can't wait to see.

Her

I felt comfortable with her.
I was unkind to her.
Was this the beginning
of my own tragedy?
Do her ghosts follow me?
She had a husband in the garden
I never wanted to replace.
I think she knew.
She can get rid of some
beatdown smitten kid
instead of feeling rejected.
We had a really good time or two,
She got to be young and beautiful
or strong and powerful.
I got to be chased after
or feel seductive and cool.
Later, I got a poem,
now two.

One Night

She had lived longer
and had promises,
but that one night
we drank from each other
until the lights went dark.
She held my eyes
as we danced deeply.
We kissed in the car.
We played in the park
and knocked over scarecrows,
soaked ourselves in tequila
and left each other high.
Then another man introduced himself
and she returned to the night.
The eagle sang a wailing song
as I fell down rocky cliffs.

Spilt

What it feels like to come down
from the tip top
of a good day
or a string of days
or even weeks
without your feet
ever touching the ground,
I am a container
dropped on the floor,
slid under the ottoman,
laying on my side,
uncapped,
and spilling out
whatever was giving me
substance.
It hurts
a kind of vague
decentralized pain
that starts in my gut
or my head...
no...
now I'm not sure
but it's all in my head
a part of my body still
but people will tell you
there's a difference.
What do I know?
I use hand soap on my face
and just go on like
everything is fine.

The Collector

for Tim Heerdink

He doesn't just collect
board games.
He studies them,
not just their rules
but every facet
the history,
each edition's
changes in design.
He meets the creators
and becomes
a part of their lives
on a first name basis.

He doesn't just collect
board games.
He reveres them.

He doesn't just collect
poets.
He learns their
quirks and styles
and hypes them up
and gets them traveling
for miles and miles
for an evening's worth
of reading and glowing
just to get back in the car
and do it again another night,
another showing.

He becomes a much appreciated
part of their lives.

Often is said

I hope Tim
can make it.

He doesn't just collect
poets.

He inspires them.

Factory Made

No one made Andy.
The kids made dreams,
and Andy threaded labels
each as beautiful and cool
as Hollywood cigarettes
with image and style.
The label said Warhol.
The kids saw
that Andy was a vampire
and loved him for it.

Tim Heerdink

The average person spends
twenty-six years of their life asleep
and another seven
just trying to get there;

it's a good thing I'm not normal.

Postmodern Mausoleum

after William Sovern after Charlie Newman

When I release myself of these exhausted bones
either through self-mutilation or by natural cause,
construct me a magnificent tomb of endless wonder
where this dead fucking flesh will remain above ground
& all the words I couldn't find can simply slip away.

Soundtrack to a Mental Breakdown

Enter scene.

A soft beginning with low bass drum
pitter-patter like a heart gone metronome
laying the foundation for the rest.

Wait, oh, there's the bassist
also low in tone but building
with its steady rhythm.

Calm, be quiet.

You don't want to miss
the wakening of guitars,
keys alongside keeping up.

This is nice;
I could be here
for a while.

Such harmo—

Trumpets roaring in an attempt
to outdo the crash of cymbals
skipping any crescendo
now forte.

I'm surely awake
if I wasn't already before.

The amount of time
it took for my mind to realize
it had but long been lost.

Suicide Note Revised

Dear those who find this letter with no corpse nearby,
I'm doing my best Jesus impersonation
& I'd appreciate it if you could leave
some feedback for me underneath these words.

On occasion, I do make plans to die,
but there's so much in this existence
that I don't want to miss out on.

It'd be a shame to never taste
a $37 milkshake
let alone a piece of cake
from France
which will cause you
to take out a second mortgage.

If I could have one of my lines
tattooed on an adoring fan
or perhaps my initials
branded by a stalker
who may finish me
off before I can,
perhaps
it'd be easier
to enter
sleep.

I Used to Think

I used to think
that I knew darkness
until the night
my journey took me
to Belle, Missouri.

I used to think
there was always
someone to blame
other than me.

I used to think
people didn't die
young, but I've been
proven otherwise.

I used to think
all the shit happened
only to me,
yet now I see
everyone suffers.

I used to think
there was no light
waiting in the distance;
oh how I was wrong.

I used to think
after my mouth
found itself open,
& I must apologize.

I used to think
before thinking
became too much
like unnecessary
trouble.

It Was Their First Time

for Jonathan S Baker

There's work to be done
& little time to spare,
but let us have a bit
of fun before
the sun begins
to rise.

Nemesis!

AKA Alien: The Board Game

A bookseller and two poets
trying to find their way
off an intruder-infested ship
with secrets running deep.

Sneaking a glimpse at my objective
like old Jesus on the World Poker Tour,
I make a plan to kill Jonathan.

Figuring them for a novice
breaking their Nemesis cherry
on a solemn autumn night,
odds are they'll have no issue
finding a way toward the exit
without my persuasion.

Curiosity causes me to check
on Sam & his motives;
good luck with that,
good fellow.

As I predicted,
Baker's soldier finds
their premature end.

They reveal
the way to victory
is to die.

We all perished on that ship
with my breath taken
by the queen.

I tried to be a good guy
once they were out of my way;
Sam just wouldn't listen!

One simply does not
walk into a corridor,
pass, & take the cake.

As is truth in life
is truth on the board;
we're all gonna die!

That Old Man from Owensboro

for Joseph Fulkerson

Last words left at the mic stand
unplugged & put away for the night
at The Spot where poetic minds
can come uncensored & spew.

Our great host rides horses unseen,
writes haiku, & harnesses electricity
like he's the god of thunder among us.

All this inspiring's got me grumbling
for a wonderful slice; say Joe,
want to come with?

Nah, I'm awful tired.

Tell me why we stood another hour
maybe another half more
out in evening's dark belly
when those booths begged
& begged for some conversation
while Baker and I made
a mess of ourselves.

Thin Ice

Things are getting a bit hot
up in this discussion
like a Dutch apple pie
tucked safely in the oven.

Who's got that vanilla bean?

There's certain topics
you just don't press
unless your armor is strong
& your tongue respectable.

Fuck me.

Throwing chairs like
I'm Steve Wilkos,
& there's no need
for you to stand.

Something
you'll discover;
I don't take well
to being
cut off.

Gwyneth Paltrow's Got a New Candle

Shew!   *What stinks?*

        Oh, that's just   the scent of
feminine independence   making a buck
        in our capitalistic   society.

I heard   you can capture
        any type of smell
& recreate it   for the masses.

        Leave it   up to Gwyneth
to bring this reality   of vaginal displeasure.

Who woulda' thunk   selling that funk
        for three-fourths   a Benjamin
                could see   out of stock notices
from those seeking   something
        out   of   the   ordinary?

Literature?

To break down the definition,
literature is *writing formed with letters*,
so those elitists can calm down
because I am not putting out a picture book.

Not yet, anyway.

It is said that the literature of a culture should reflect
with elegance and intelligence
the values of the times.

No genre writing is to be included.
Sorry, Mr. King,
but horrors from the likes of *Carrie* and *Misery*
just do not cut the standard.
We shall overlook the fact
that this man cranks these things out like hotcakes,
and many are bestsellers.

So, what if I used a cliché?
Writing should come from within.
I don't do it just for you.
It is uplifting to know that King finally was acknowledged,
receiving a literary award from the President.
Maybe one does not have to be dead
or a one hit wonder
to be considered a writer of literature.
Who is to say that a town under a dome
or a girl who can light fires with her mind
cannot be eloquent?

May it be ordinary or extraordinary,
I consider it all to be literature.

Their Eyes Were Watching Her

At a distance,
every man's tide turns away
in his dreams
mocked to death by Time.
Now,
don't remember
the dream is the truth.
Act accordingly.

So,
a woman had come back
from burying the dead.
Sick friends had returned
from beyond the earth.
Their eyes saw her.
The sun was gone.
It was time to talk.
Tongueless, earless, eyeless brutes.
Their skins, now the sun,
were so powerful
and human.
Lords of lesser things
passed their judgment.
Seeing envy stored up
with relish,
killing was like harmony.

Coming back here
blue,
where she had died
and left.

To End Your Life, Press 1

Advancements in the science of medicine
keep people alive and depressed.
With the mortality rate ever-changing,
more are coming in than going out,
which causes the threat of a world
where overpopulation forces its occupants
to starve, thirst, and be claustrophobic.
Tiny capsules designed to extend this existence
only create a new problem with a tough solution.
America will be committing infanticide
just like those from the land who make everything.
Mothers will carry their screaming children into the woods
and never look back.

42

Eventually,
people may get the idea to stop fucking
without thinking
and slow the flooding waters of humanity
like a little Dutch boy with his finger in a hole.
Temptation has its way, though.
Even Jesus can attest.

So,
another option will be drawn up.
Don't you fret.
It's as simple as tapping fingers on a screen;
waiting for relief to come with a dial tone.
Perhaps the line shall be connected to a drone
or a chip inside your head.
If it is your wish
to be dead,
please press 1.

In Search of the Wolf

Fie, fie, fie!
I know your name,
and now I must testify.
Your kind tells lies and hides
amidst the innocence
worshipping in this holy place.
Show your face,
deceiver of the night!
Be gone with your wicked ways.
Bother us no more.

43

Inability to Shoot

Sometimes, I cannot shoot.
Not when it comes to .22
but when it comes to Chapter 2.
I can knock them all down when it comes to the pins.
Several come close,
but I am the one who wins.
If only it were that easy to get my thoughts straight.
Maybe I can blame my hands because they ache.
Starting over always seems to be a waste.
My only wish is to break this scheme.
It's tiring to know that I am my obstacle.
The gun is loaded and I am ready to shoot.
Perhaps this time I won't miss.
Letters will fly like bullets to the paper.
All of it will make sense,
but I will revise and make it better.
No years of loathing and regret for stalling.
Not this time,
for I have hit my bull's eye,
and there is no end in sight.

44

10202021

Today, I discovered
I have a superpower.

Yes, you can call me
a superhero of sorts.

Not all of us wear capes,
though it's under consideration.

What's my power
you ask?

Well, it just so
happens to be evasion.

Evasion of recognition,
of them dreaded awards.

I have an invisibility cloak
so them cats don't see me.

Don't worry about titles,
these words are for you.

If I got a nomination or won,
it'd be a sign my cover's been blown.

& there's only one way
I want to be blown.

Clockwork

Tick-tock, tick-tock.

Good-bye, my thoughts.
How is anyone supposed to concentrate
when it's just minutes before noon
and all you want to do is fill
the void inside you with food?

That circular tormentor on the wall
with its hands up
like it is about to get shot
by a cop whose britches are just too big.
Just too trigger-happy to be
a symbol of peace.
Maybe I should watch out
as I go out to eat.

Perhaps I will be driven by my hunger to feast,
which triggers my lead foot to become heavy.
The sign says sixty,
but I am going seventy.
Red and blue illuminations in my rear-view
and soon I discover that the sirens
are not a part of my tune.
Hopefully,
he does not get antsy
when he sees that I have a license which is pink
and backup underneath my seat.

Stopped on the side of the street,
I see Mister Brown Pants
all high and mighty
coming toward me.

I would like to say,
Fuck you, asshole!

but instead,
I put on my fake face,
which seems to be my only face
anymore.

The Penis Poet's Had Enough

for Jonathan S Baker

Sitting in a lounge chair
beside the speakers in Bokeh,
I find out the Penis Poet
has finally snapped.

They've had enough
of the bullshit.

All the voices
that used to be
in their head
have overflowed
to the back table.

With my eardrum blown,
Jonathan starts their set
with demonic screams
like a rocker in Hell.

That shut them up
for about the time
it takes for one shot
of whiskey
to be killed
before the next
marvelous stanza
could begin.

Leave My Dreams Be

More & more I despise FM radio
with its endless run of ads
like what they got is for me
when all I need is my jam.

Some afternoons while on break,
those guitar chords opening
one of my favorite Cranberries tunes
reach across the room & make me smile.

For some fucked up reason,
a chick with the station feels
this instrumental intro is perfect
for her to blab about stupid shit
until Dolores can finally shut her up
& remind me that even from the grave
her words & her voice have worth.

49

Hell Dimension

Sterile linoleum squeaking under shoe
in hallways & doors with no rooms
stands a line which moves yet
never appears to make progress.

Voids cut triangles in clavicles
creating an entryway to emptiness
each individual hopes will fill
once numbers on their sheet ring.

This place does not breathe eternal flame
nor can it house all fallen horned creatures
for they must appear pretty to sway you
from shallows toward black lakes' deep.

You can cross yourself & whisper upward,
but the time for repentance of sin has passed
& holy connection line no longer shows a tone
within Hell's walls where you'll forever be alone.

May They Live Long Lives

Despite my appearance,
I am not very close
with a lot of my extended family.

It seems ways part with the loss
we experience with matriarchs.

My grandma died at 74,
my mom at 57,
& I look at what's left
thinking that these people
who don't care about me
better live a long time
just to prove it can be done.

That my genetics have the strength
to make it to a ripe old age;
if not for myself
for my daughters.

I've had some make it to late eighties,
even 93 for old Elwood,
my great grandpa
who ate as he pleased
& lived a fulfilled life;
let's get back to that.

Explicit

after Greg Leach

When I die,
I want everyone to know
the man they're mourning
was as true as they come.

My many faces hidden within
come out in each setting
no matter who is around.

You know if I like you or not.

I'm that Holocaust guy,
but I also think
of ending things
despite the inconvenience.

This death won't be a walk in the woods
but a final descent in the ocean
with the heavy stones I carry
in my pockets & a .22 in my hand.

No,
I hope to live
a long time
until I'm ready to die.

We can't all live forever.

Making That Market Drop

In the spot where Heritage dips
stands a most vile house
owned by a lady
who only wears a robe
& smokes on her stoop
all day long.

If you so happen to pass,
she'll wave at you
because she knows
you're staring.

Up until last week,
those windows showed
she was a hoarder
with walls up to the ceiling
packed beyond capacity.

A turn of events has seen
this massive collection
extracted from its prison
for full display on the outside.

It's almost like a game
to see how unpleasant
one can possibly be.

The neighbors are trying
their best to escape,
but even this market
proves not to be
in their favor.

Out of work
& in her forties or so,
this collector has a house
of kids of all colors and sizes.

One is about three
& is only ever in a diaper
outside by the road.

There are at least
four or five more
who help sustain
her particular lifestyle.

I have to wonder
if any or all
are hers,
& how
she's seen
to be fit
for care.

The latest addition
beside a pop-up tent
that's always set up
for a yard sale never meant to be
is a grand cage
to hold aluminum cans
like she'll ever recycle.

We all know
she's laughing
& proud.

There's bound to be
at least five dead cats
stuck somewhere
on that property.

In the back is a Pomeranian
encaged in weeds taller than itself;
the rest of the yard remains
cut short so others can't file
a report on the landscaping.

I want to know
what they're
distracting us from.

Are there bodies
in the basement?

Nothing surprises me anymore.

What They Want You to Believe

Australia is real
the earth is round
you have purpose
it wasn't an inside job
a man landed on the moon
those *"Australians"* aren't actors
Mandela didn't die way back when
there's such a thing as privacy
we are free
there's no chance we'll end up
like those British criminals
dead in the sea
it didn't happen, anyway
nobody falls off the tails side
except maybe the Australians,
because they do in fact exist
the elections are fair
every vote counts
just look how they do it
in Australia

Us Motherless Men

I woke up just before eight on a Sunday
without a voice singing *Happy Birthday*
at that time when I entered this existence.

Everyone in their beds while I scooched
past the pooch to stare at the older man
staring back at me in that dim night light.

There's a growing list of acquaintances
who find this celebration hard for grins
as we travel along, us motherless men.

I Thought I Saw John Dorsey

for John Dorsey

In the mix of the crowd,
I thought I saw the hair.

Through the darkness
of a mere moment
stood here in Indiana,
this land of corn & meth,
a poet
friend
lover of fried chicken
the man himself,
John Dorsey.

I thought I saw John Dorsey
with a chap in one hand
& maybe a wing in the other.

It was hard to tell in my confusion.

Sure,
the guy gets around,
but wouldn't he give a ring
first?

I could be wrong
as I often am,
but I swear
on the lives
of chickens
everywhere
I thought I saw John Dorsey;
they better prepare themselves.

Avert Your Eyes, That's Not a Sunset, The World is Aflame

It may look beautiful & you may want to stare,
but that's not the collection of colors
pollution creates over years
spilling into the atmosphere.

So many of our kind
are taking their last breath
in this descending sequence.

Paintbrush stroking splats of orange
across the canvas with rhythmic flicks
as fires feed their appetites with the landscape.

The collective screams sound like birds
flying off in the distance toward south
in a song of farewell to good friends.

We knew this night would come,
we just never thought it'd be
within our own hundred years.

It'll be a matter of minutes
before the end comes,
you can choose to run
for the cover which
does not exist;
I'll take in
the view.

About the Authors

Jonathan S Baker lives and works in Evansville, Indiana alongside their dog and is overwhelmed by guilt and anxiety. They are the author of *Cock of the Walk* (**Laughing Ronin Press**) and *Flowers for Forrest* (**Last Lights Press**). They are also the co-editor of **The Grind Stone** and the editor-in-chief at **Pure Sleeze Press**.

Tim Heerdink collects board games, poets (sometimes he feeds them), and answers to the world's problems (which he forgets to write down in the morning). He is the author of *Final Flight as the Fog Becomes Night* (**impspired**), *Somniloquy & Trauma in the Knottseau Well* (**Cajun Mutt Press**), *The Human Remains* (**Bird Brain Publishing**), and eight chapbooks. He is co-editor of **The Grind Stone**, editor-in-chief of **Last Lights Press**, and the President of the **Midwest Writers Guild** (of Evansville, Indiana).

Gratitude

Sam and Adam Morris for getting this project started

John Dorsey and Victor Clevenger for lighting that poetic fire and inspiring others to stick with the craft

William "Hoosier Bill" Sovern for making connections at Bokeh Lounge in Evansville, Indiana. All Hail the Horsemen!

Tony Brewer, Joseph Fulkerson, and Jon Koker those Horsemen who didn't write any poems in this book, but probably inspired all of them

Amber, Audrey, and Auria who created a female world for an untrained man to live in

Fevers of the Mind; The Crossroads Magazine; A Thin Slice of Anxiety; Versification Zine; Trailer Park Quarterly; Alien Buddha Press; Seppuku Quarterly; The Notes Will Carry Me Home; Tickets to Midnight and other fine presses of exemplary taste who have previously published poems from this book.

Arizona if not for the preservation of sanity, then for embracing eccentricities.

Each Other the poets are blessed by mutual admiration, inspiration, and assistance